The Tria[thlon]

by Michèle Dufresne

Literacy Footprints, Inc.

Table of Contents

Getting Ready. 4

Triathletes. 8

Swimming. 12

Cycling. 16

Running. 18

Glossary. 24

Index. 24

Getting Ready

Here is Nick.

Nick is going to compete in a triathlon.
A triathlon is an athletic event
made up of three sports:
swimming, bicycling, and running.

Nick is getting ready to go to Switzerland for a World Championship triathlon competition.

A triathlete must be very fit. All three events are **endurance** sports.

To get ready, Nick must practice for long hours. He swims, rides his bike, and runs everyday. It is hard work!

Triathletes

Finally, it is race day.

Nick arrives early, long before the race will begin. He picks a spot in the **transition** area. This is the place where the athletes will change their clothes and shoes, and park their bicycles.

There are two kinds of triathletes:
the **professional** triathlete,
and the **amateur** triathlete.

A professional triathlete earns money for racing and competes with other professional triathletes. Amateur triathletes compete with other amateur triathletes in their age group.

Nick is an amateur triathlete.
He will race with other amateur triathletes who are 20-24 years old.

Swimming

After Nick sets up in the transition area, he puts on his swim gear.

Triathletes swim in pools, lakes, rivers, and oceans. The swimming part of this World Championship triathlon
is taking place in Lake Geneva.

There are many athletes
at the World Championship. Athletes have come
from all over the world to race.

The competitors for each age group enter
the water together at the signal.
There will be groups of athletes entering
the water every few minutes.

Nick swims as fast as he can!

Cycling

After they have finished swimming, the triathletes hurry out of the water. Nick runs and changes into his cycling gear as fast as he can. He takes off his goggles, and puts on his helmet and his cycling shoes.

Nick starts the 24-mile bike race.

He cycles as fast as he can,
up and down the hills.
He tucks his arms into his **aerobars**
to speed up his ride.

Running

The last event in the triathlon is running.

Nick leaves his bike in the transition area.
He takes off his cycling shoes
and puts on his running shoes.
He is tired and hot.
After a quick drink, he begins to run.

The running **course** is marked so none of the racers will get lost.

There are people set up along the way, giving out water to the thirsty athletes.

At the end of the race, Nick is tired.
He is also very happy. He worked hard, and raced against some of the best athletes in the world.

He is a world-class athlete!

Glossary

aerobars: special handle bars designed to reduce wind drag

amateur: a person who does a sport or activity without getting paid

course: the route of a competition with a starting point and an end point

endurance: the ability to keep up a difficult effort for a long time

professional: an athlete who is paid to compete in the sport

transition: to change from one activity to another

Index

cycling 4, 6, 16, 17
running 4, 6, 18, 19, 20, 21

swimming 4, 6, 12, 13, 14, 15